drawn dreams

Your wildest dreams are drawn to you—since they're drawn by you.
Maddie-Jo

All rights reserved. No part of this publication may be reproduced, distributed, or transmitted in any form or by any means, including photocopying, recording, or other electronic or mechanical methods without the prior written permission of the publisher except for brief quotations embodied in critical reviews.

Copyright © 2018 by Maddie-Jo Anderson

DrawnDreams.com

@DrawnDream5

978-1-7752164-1-4
First Edition

"Drawn Dreams is the law of attraction, applied."
— Teresa L. DeCicco, PhD

ACKNOWLEDGMENTS

Words can't express how grateful I am for my soul mate, Chase. Thank you for your heaps of love, patience, and support during this journey. I also thank my wise and loving parents, Joe and Penny-Claire. Chase, mom, and dad, you three are my biggest teachers. Thank you for lifting me up, believing in me, and being my fellow dreamers.

I will be forever grateful for my supportive friends, my best friend Brittany Lengauer, the lovely Tuckky Kulisara, Tyler Tilley, and my extended family, as well as my inspiring social media tribe.

Teresa DeCicco, thank you so much for your helpful guidance through this process.

Thank you to my incredible editor, Josie Ferguson. I also want to thank Romeo Mario for the gorgeous illustrations.

Listya Nindita, I'm so thankful for your amazing design and your help with bringing Drawn Dreams to life.

I must also thank the great Oprah Winfrey for impacting my life in such a positive way. It was on your epic talk show where I first heard of gratitude journaling. The very first episode of The Oprah Winfrey Show aired three days after I was born, so I can honestly say, you've been steeping my soul with wisdom and "Aha" moments my whole life.

Last but not least, my thanks goes to you. Thanks for being open-minded enough to open this book and see what Drawn Dreams is all about.

DEDICATION

I dedicate Drawn Dreams to my two brilliant brothers.
Spencer Dean Tillapaugh (aka "Snips"), my younger brother, who now lives in heaven, and Tyler Jesse Tillapaugh (Tyler Tilley) who lives off his art sales in Thailand.

It was Snips who said: "I'm grateful that I'm grateful."

If it wasn't for you brothers, I would have never been inspired to move abroad and think of this gratitude sketching idea.

You both encourage me, are always there for me, and continue to make me smile and laugh.

May your kind, creative, fun, loving legacies live on—for infinity.

I love you, Spencer. I love you, Tyler.

Drive: This loving investment in yourself puts you on the right track. It provides the drive you need to create a great day—a day to be grateful for.

Reflection: A daily reflection that helps you to appreciate the blessings lighting up your life in that moment. It's fun to flip back through sketches to reflect on and give you an instant mood booster.

Art: Sketching, a form of art therapy, is a great stress reliever. Unleash this playful, high frequency energy inside you.

Woohoo!! It's a warm, positive, empowering and uplifting activity for your well-being, making you feel more confident, radiant, and wonderful.

Nourishing: Nourish your soul and your grieving heart.

Discovery: More gratitude will appear. You will discover more and more blessings in your life, on a day-to-day basis.

Refresh: A clear and calming, soul-quenching kick-start to your day.

Educate: Learn more about yourself, what's important to you, how you can serve others, and what you enjoy. Embrace what you uncover about your authentic self.

Awareness: A self-love and higher consciousness tool to check in spiritually. You'll feel connected with a sense of oneness. This book encourages you to be present, mindful, and aware of your feelings, energy, and surroundings.

Manifest: Witness and celebrate as your hopes, intentions, and dreams materialize.

Surprise: Allow the big and little gifts, that gratitude brings, surprise you.

INTRO

I first learned the magic of writing my goals down at age 11. I have continued to create and record personal goals since then because the results are so dramatic and inspiring.

In 1998, it started out as a fun family activity. We encouraged each other to dream and record dozens of goals every New Year's Day. A year later on January 1st, we would share our success stories with joy and amazement. Then we would create new goals and dreams for the year ahead. It is a beautiful family tradition that continues to this day.

As many of us are aware, visualization is a creative behavior that facilitates goal achievement. With Drawn Dreams, not only are you setting goals, but you're visualizing them through your drawings. This combination, immersed in gratitude and on a daily basis, works wonders for me. It lifts my spirits and materializes my dreams. It's a ritual that welcomes a day filled with joyous opportunities. I am so delighted to share this discovery because I know it will work for you too.

My late brother Spencer was really into the Rhonda Byrne books The Secret and The Magic, which were also an inspiration to me when creating Drawn Dreams. The two books are all about the Law of Attraction as well as Gratitude. Spencer once wrote in his journal: "I'm grateful that I'm grateful"—words I now live by.

The other quote that has struck home with me the most is from David Steindl-Rast:
"It is not joy that makes us grateful, it is gratitude that makes us joyful." Being grateful and therefore happy is what Drawn Dreams is all about.

This daily gratitude sketching idea came through me when I was living by the sea in County Cork, Ireland. Before this idea I was stressed, depressed, and I didn't want to be on this earth anymore. Drawn Dreams lifts my spirits every day, nourishes my soul, and inspires me to be my authentic self. Also, the more I draw my dreams, the more dreams are drawn to me. Therefore, friend, I recommend you draw on a daily basis.

Let's be grateful for life, now, and be grateful for our manifestations being drawn to us.

Love,
Maddie-Jo

DRAWN DREAMS DIRECTIONS

1
Begin your daily entry by attributing your thanks.
Fill in the blank and give thanks to the universe and/or your higher power.

For Example:
Thank You *God*

2
Fill in the date.

3
Below you will find the Gratitude Sketching Space, your canvas, where you can let your inner child shine. Draw what you are grateful for.

This should include what you are currently blessed with and what you want to be blessed with.
From the cup of joe you're sipping on (I tend to draw steaming coffee cups a lot), to your dream home.
There is no goal too big or too small, and there is no blessing too insignificant to draw.

DRAWN DREAMS TIPS

Manifestation Sketches: Drawing Your Dreams

Details
When drawing your hopes and dreams, the more details the better.
For example: Does your dream home have a hot tub, and are you in the hot tub with your partner? Do you have two sweet-smelling rose bushes by the front door of your dream home? Do you have friendly neighbors with big smiles?

Visualize
Envision what you draw. Picture yourself having the thing that you want, and think about how it feels to achieve this dream.

Gratitude
Out loud, give a heartfelt "thank you" to the universe or to your higher power as you draw your dream.

Believe
Be grateful for your drawn dreams now by trusting and believing they are part of your present life already.

Let it Go
You see it, you radiate gratitude, you believe, now let it go. Trust the universe is working in your favor.

GIVE THANKS TO ALL SKETCHES

For any item drawn, spend at least 30 seconds being thankful for it. Take time to feel your heart, holding it with one or two hands.

Let yourself smile and feel warm and fuzzy as you let your gratitude fill up your heart.

Allow yourself to truly appreciate the blessing and give thanks to the universe, life itself, or your higher power. This book is intended to be a fun mood booster, so remember to be loving and easy on yourself. Get creative, laugh at what you draw, and share your drawings with your loved ones.

Some days you may only be grateful for one thing, and it may only take you 10 seconds to draw. That is great, but do take a moment to notice what it feels like to be grateful for having that one thing in your life.

MAKE GRATITUDE A HABIT

Draw at a similar moment each day, to make Drawn Dreams a part of your routine. You'll want to pick a time in your day most convenient for you. You may find you have to set a reminder for the first several days.

Some solid dream drawing times are: each morning with your coffee (that's what I do), during your lunch hour, right after dinner, right before you start watching a show or movie in the evening, or in bed right before you hit the hay.

SKETCHING INSPIRATIONS

On most pages, you will find an example dream illustration to keep those wheels turning.

On the next few pages, you will see daily entry examples to see how others have used their books.

GRATITUDE TOPICS

Below are some additional ideas on what you could sketch—aspects in your life to be grateful for and to improve:

Things that make you smile; fun, recreational activities; health; wealth; happiness; relationships; partner; friends; family; home; career; freedom; running water; salary; travel; fitness; spirituality; confidence; legacy; contribution; possessions; forgiveness; issues to be solved; tasks to do; education; a loved one's well-being; gratitude from previous day(s); volunteering; smiling at strangers.

Thank You Universe! !
Thank you GOD!

Date: May 25th

Thank You

Date: Nov. 27

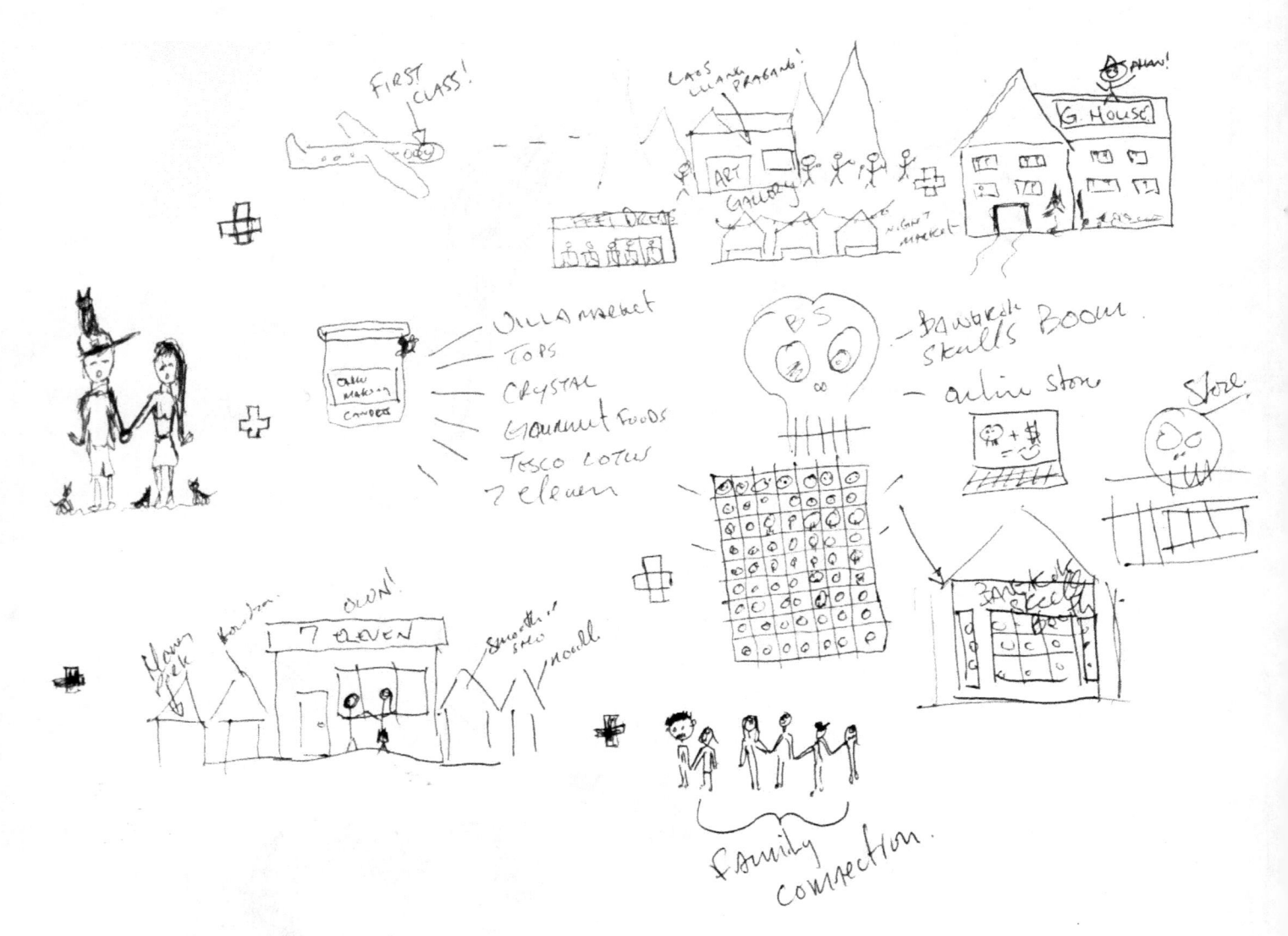

Thank You God   Date: Dec 19th

Dream On

Having read the previous directions please know this is your journal, your canvas, and each day you can use it any way you feel.

It's your turn, now.
Have fun!

Thank You
Maddie-Jo

Date: DEC 15th 2018

Hope

love

Thank You   **Date:**

Thank You   **Date:**

Thank You   **Date:**

—— *On today's Drawn Dreams canvas, draw what you really enjoy doing. What are activities that light you up?*

Thank You   **Date:**

Thank You   **Date:**

Thank You   **Date:**

—— *What is something that happened, in the last 24 hours, that you appreciate? Draw it below.*

Positive Affirmations are positive statements you tell yourself. Reciting them is said to help you achieve anything and create the reality you want.

Every several days/pages you will find an Affirmation Section. This is where you're encouraged to customize a positive saying just for you. You will find an affirmation with space underneath; if you choose, you are welcome to write your own helpful mantra in that space.

These hopeful sentences are used for personal growth and empowerment, so write them in first person ("I"). With this book, we're striving to live in the present moment so your affirmations should be in present tense.
For example, don't say: "I will be grateful."
Do say: "I am grateful."

When you've finished customizing your personal declaration, say it out loud several times to yourself with conviction.

From my experience, affirmations are beneficial because they train my brain to think in a positive manner. The way I view and speak about myself, others, and situations are much more loving, open, and positive. Plus, I just feel terrific after reciting them.

Thank You   **Date:**

Affirmations: I let go of all fear and replace this with love.
_____
_____
_____

Thank You   **Date:**

—— *What are three things you love about yourself? Draw them below.*

Thank You　　　　　　　　　　　　　　　　　　　　　　　　　　　　　　**Date:**

Thank You   **Date:**

Thank You   Date:

Thank You   **Date:**

Thank You   **Date:**

Affirmations: I accept myself the way I am. I am enough.
_____
_____
_____
_____

Thank You   Date:

Thank You   **Date:**

Thank You   **Date:**

Thank You   **Date:**

—— *What is a fun activity you would like to do with a friend(s)? Include it on your canvas below.*

Thank You **Date:**

Affirmations: I am a great listener.

Thank You   **Date:**

Thank You Date:

Thank You 　　　　　　　　　　　　　　　　　　　　　　　　　　　　　**Date:**

Affirmations: I bring happiness to every aspect of my life.
_____
_____
_____
_____

Thank You   **Date:**

Thank You   **Date:**

—— *What is something that made you smile in the last 24 hours? Sketch it below.*

Thank You   **Date:**

Thank You   **Date:**

Thank You   Date:

Thank You   **Date:**

Affirmations: My heart is happy and open.
_____
_____
_____
_____

Thank You   Date:

Thank You   **Date:**

—— *Draw a personality trait you like about yourself.*

Thank You   Date:

Thank You   **Date:**

You are quite the artist.
Support and see other inspiring interpretations of the Drawn Dreams' canvas.

Share your gratitude art on Instagram, Twitter, or Facebook with the hashtag:
#DrawnDreams.

Thank You   Date:

Thank You   **Date:**

Thank You   **Date:**

—— *Include a sketch of someone you are grateful for today.*

Thank You   **Date:**

—— *What is something that happened to you when you were a child that you appreciate? Include it in today's sketch.*

Thank You Date:

Thank You   **Date:**

Affirmations: It'll be good, or it'll be good – Tyler Tilley, artist.
_____
_____
_____
_____

Thank You   **Date:**

You Have Drawn Dreams
Let's flip back through your book to see what has come to fruition.
Feel free to use a different colored writing utensil and circle or put a checkmark beside what has come true.

Now draw these great things that have come into your life and express your gratitude.

Thank You   **Date:**

Thank You Date:

Thank You   **Date:**

Thank You   **Date:**

Affirmations: My body keeps getting healthier and stronger.
_____
_____
_____
_____

Thank You   **Date:**

Thank You   **Date:**

—— *What do you want to attract more of in your beautiful life? Draw it below.*

Thank You Date:

Thank You   **Date:**

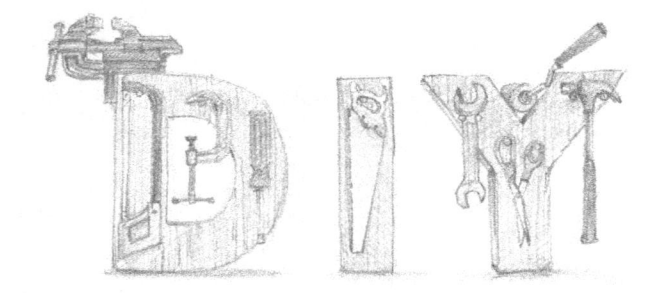

Thank You   Date:

DIY

Thank You   **Date:**

Affirmations: I am blessed with wonderful, loving connections.
_____
_____
_____
_____

Thank You   **Date:**

Affirmations: I trust the flow of life, and I listen and watch for guidance.
_____
_____
_____
_____

Thank You   Date:

Thank You   **Date:**

Thank You   **Date:**

—— *What is something you could do to make your next 24 hours more meaningful? Sketch it below.*

Thank You   **Date:**

Thank You   Date:

Thank You   **Date:**

——— *What awesomeness do you see for yourself 10 years from now? Draw it all below.*

Thank You   **Date:**

Thank You Date:

Affirmations: Everything I need now is here.
_____
_____
_____
_____

Thank You   **Date:**

Thank You   **Date:**

Affirmations: I am honest, I am real, I am authentically me.
_____
_____
_____
_____

Thank You   Date:

Thank You   **Date:**

—— *What is something you've always wanted to do or learn? Sketch yourself doing it.*

Thank You   **Date:**

Thank You   **Date:**

Thank You   **Date:**

Thank You   **Date:**

Thank You   **Date:**

Affirmations: I have a safe bubble around me.
_____
_____
_____
_____

Thank You   **Date:**

Thank You　　　　　　　　　　　　　　　　　　　　　　　　　　　　　**Date:**

Affirmations: I deserve to be paid well for my time, efforts, and ideas.
_____
_____
_____
_____

Thank You   Date:

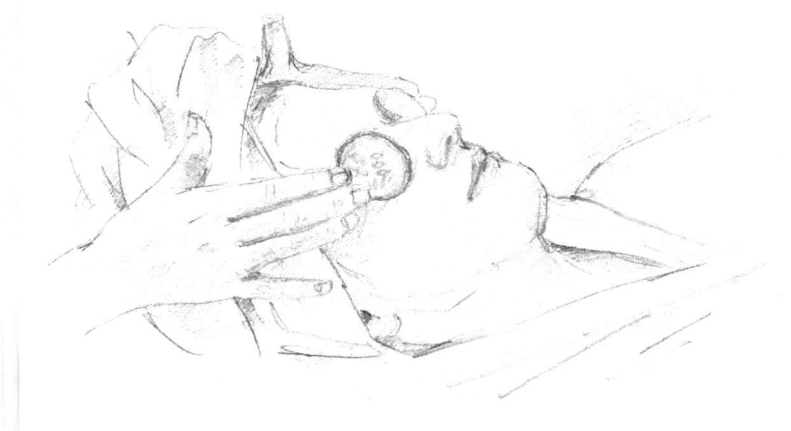

Thank You   Date:

Thank You   **Date:**

—— *Draw yourself financially free. What are you doing with your abundance of money? Where in the world are you? Who are you with?*

Thank You   **Date:**

Affirmations: I am a money magnet.
_____
_____
_____
_____

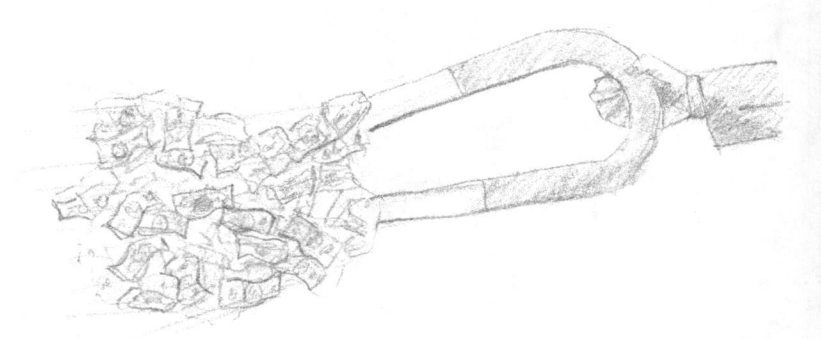

Thank You   **Date:**

Thank You   **Date:**

Thank You   **Date:**

Thank You   **Date:**

Thank You   **Date:**

—— *Sketch something that makes you laugh.*

Thank You   **Date:**

Thank You   **Date:**

Thank You **Date:**

Affirmations: I see myself in everyone and everything.
_____
_____
_____
_____

Thank You   **Date:**

Thank You   Date:

Thank You   **Date:**

Affirmations: I feel comfortable, calm, and cozy.
_____
_____
_____
_____

Thank You   **Date:**

—— *Sketch something you haven't sketched yet.*

Thank You   **Date:**

Thank You   **Date:**

Thank You   **Date:**

Dreams Do Come True
Time to flip back and see what dreams have been drawn to you.
Checkmark or circle all your drawn dreams (if possible use a different colored writing utensil).

Draw the things you are now blessed with in your life, thanking the universe and/or your higher power.

Thank You   Date:

Thank You   **Date:**

Thank You   **Date:**

—— *What is one of the smaller tasks you've been putting off? Sketch yourself accomplishing that task.*

Thank You   **Date:**

Affirmations: I freely radiate my creativity and talents.
_____
_____
_____
_____

Thank You   Date:

Thank You   **Date:**

Thank You   **Date:**

Affirmations: I am free!

_____
_____
_____
_____

Thank You   **Date:**

Thank You   **Date:**

Affirmations: I love nature, and I take time to enjoy its beauty.
_____
_____
_____
_____

Thank You   **Date:**

—— *What is something you need today (or over the next 24 hours)? A hug? A phone call with a family member or a friend? Include that in today's sketch.*

Thank You   **Date:**

Thank You									Date:

Thank You   **Date:**

Thank You   **Date:**

Thank You   **Date:**

Affirmations: Inhale: dreams. Exhale: gratitude.

_____
_____
_____
_____

Thank You   Date:

Thank You   **Date:**

Thank You   Date:

Thank You   **Date:**

—— *How do you wind down or relieve stress in a healthy way? Draw yourself performing that activity.*

Thank You   **Date:**

Thank You   **Date:**

Thank You Date:

Thank You   **Date:**

Thank You   **Date:**

Affirmations: In this very moment, I am overflowing with gratitude.
_____
_____
_____
_____

Thank You   **Date:**

Thank You Date:

Affirmations: My life's purpose brings me prosperity and joy.
_____
_____
_____
_____

Thank You   Date:

Thank You　　　　　　　　　　　　　　　　　　　　　　　　　　　　　　**Date:**

Thank You   Date:

Thank You   **Date:**

Affirmations: I am open and receive the abundance of money flowing in.
_____
_____
_____
_____

Thank You   **Date:**

Thank You   **Date:**

Thank You	Date:

Thank You   **Date:**

Affirmations: I respect my mind, body, and spirit.
_____
_____
_____
_____

Thank You   **Date:**

—— *Who's someone that you want to spend more time with? Draw yourself with that person, and give thanks for them.*

Thank You   **Date:**

Thank You   **Date:**

Thank You   **Date:**

Thank You   **Date:**

Affirmations: I love me. I love me. I love me.
_____
_____
_____
_____

Thank You   **Date:**

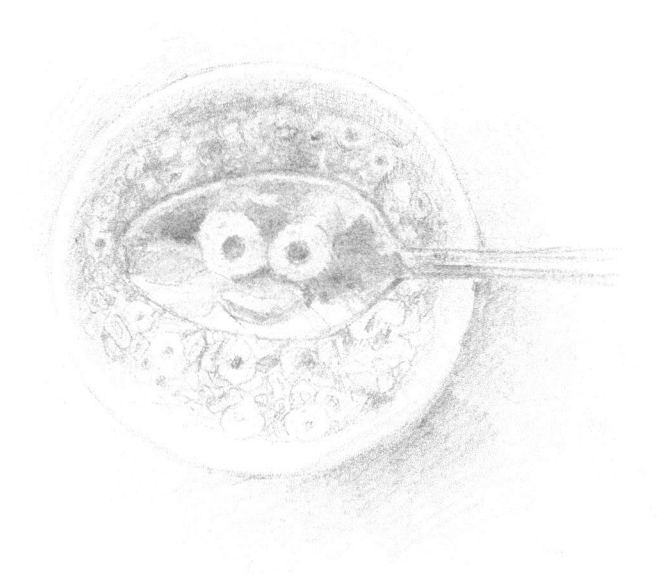

Thank You   **Date:**

Thank You　　　　　　　　　　　　　　　　　　　　　　　**Date:**

Thank You   **Date:**

Thank You   **Date:**

—— *Draw something that you like about yourself, that you haven't drawn yet.*

Thank You   Date:

Thank You   **Date:**

Affirmations: I am generous.
_____
_____
_____
_____

Thank You				Date:

Thank You   **Date:**

Thank You   **Date:**

Send love, light, and positive vibes to your **#DrawnDreams** *clan!*

Get inspired by your fellow dreamers; check out other gratitude masterpieces by searching social media with the hashtag **#DrawnDreams.**

Thank You   **Date:**

Thank You   **Date:**

Affirmations: "I am perfect health." - Dr. Wayne Dyer

_____
_____
_____
_____

Thank You   **Date:**

Thank You   **Date:**

—— *What activity do you want to perform today (or over the next 24 hours)? Take a walk in nature? Buy a stranger a coffee? Enjoy a hot bath? Some stretching? Read a book? Draw it.*

Thank You   **Date:**

Thank You   Date:

Thank You   **Date:**

Thank You   **Date:**

Affirmations: I surround myself with positive, loving people.
_____
_____
_____
_____

Thank You   **Date:**

Thank You   Date:

Thank You   **Date:**

—— *Who is someone that supports you? With love and appreciation, draw them supporting you.*

Thank You

Date:

Thank You   **Date:**

Thank You   **Date:**

Affirmations: I look and feel younger and younger every day.
_____
_____
_____
_____

Thank You   Date:

You've Drawn Dreams
Take a peek back to see what dreams have been drawn your way.
Circle/checkmark your blessings (if possible, use a different colored writing utensil).

Now draw these dreams that have come to fruition and express appreciation for them.

Thank You   Date:

Thank You   **Date:**

Thank You   Date:

Thank You   **Date:**

—— *Draw a short-term goal(s) you have for yourself this week.*

Thank You   **Date:**

Affirmations: I truly deserve the life of my dreams.
_____
_____
_____
_____

Thank You **Date:**

Thank You   **Date:**

Affirmations: I am love. I am whole. I am worthy.
_____
_____
_____
_____

Thank You   Date:

Thank You   **Date:**

Thank You   **Date:**

Thank You   **Date:**

Thank You   **Date:**

Thank You   Date:

Thank You   Date:

Thank You   **Date:**

—— *Sketch yourself in a destination you've always wanted to visit.*

Thank You   **Date:**

Thank You   **Date:**

Thank You   **Date:**

Affirmations: I trust the universe.

_____
_____
_____
_____

Thank You Date:

Thank You   **Date:**

Thank You   **Date:**

Affirmations: I feel free to say "no" to others and "yes" to myself.
_____
_____
_____
_____

Thank You   **Date:**

—— *What are three sounds you are grateful for? Draw them below.*

Thank You   **Date:**

Thank You　　　　　　　　　　　　　　　　　　　　　　　　　　　　　　　**Date:**

Thank You Date:

Thank You .... **Date:**

Affirmations: I relax and allow my life to unfold.
_____
_____
_____
_____

Thank You Date:

Thank You   **Date:**

Thank You   Date:

Thank You   **Date:**

Affirmations: I am creative and driven.
_____
_____
_____
_____

Thank You   **Date:**

Thank You   **Date:**

Thank You   Date:

Thank You   **Date:**

—— *Who is somebody you want to forgive?*
Draw them and send love to that person. Say, "I forgive you, _____".

Thank You   **Date:**

Thank You   **Date:**

Thank You   **Date:**

Thank You   **Date:**

Affirmations: Every day I find time to sketch, visualize, and be grateful.
_____
_____
_____
_____

Thank You   Date:

Thank You   **Date:**

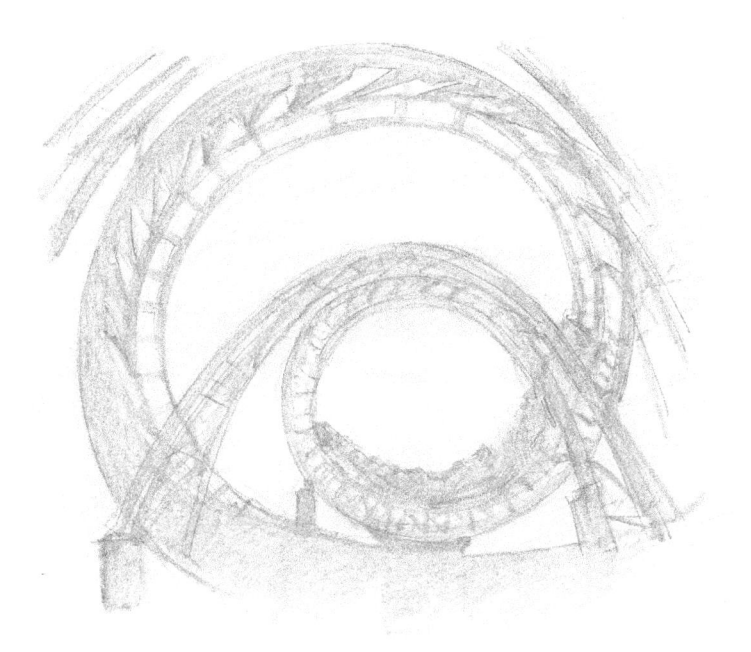

Thank You   Date:

Thank You **Date:**

Thank You   Date:

Thank You **Date:**

—— *What are three scents you are grateful for? Draw them below.*

Thank You					Date:

Thank You **Date:**

Thank You   **Date:**

Affirmations: Today I will focus on what makes me feel good.
_____
_____
_____
_____

Thank You   **Date:**

Thank You   Date:

Thank You   **Date:**

Thank You   **Date:**

Thank You   **Date:**

Thank You   **Date:**

—— *Send a gratitude note to someone today. Send appreciation to that person with a thank you text, letter, or email.*

Thank You Date:

Thank You   **Date:**

Affirmations: Every decision I make and everything I do comes from a place of love.
_____
_____
_____
_____

Thank You   **Date:**

Thank You   **Date:**

*What's your favorite gratitude sketch to draw? Share your gratitude with your Drawn Dreams fam' with the hashtag: **#DrawnDreams.***

Thank You **Date:**

Thank You   **Date:**

—— *Try to sketch a positive affirmation for yourself.*

Thank You   **Date:**

Thank You   Date:

Thank You Date:

Thank You   **Date:**

Affirmations: I'm so grateful for all I have in my life at this moment. Life is good.

_____
_____
_____
_____

Thank You   **Date:**

Drawn Dreams
Let's take a look back to see all the amazing dreams you've drawn. With a different colored pen or pencil, circle or checkmark the drawings that have come into your life.

Draw your favorite blessings on this page and express your appreciation for this abundance.

Thank You   **Date:**

I'm grateful that you're grateful.

Love,
Maddie-Jo

CPSIA information can be obtained
at www.ICGtesting.com
Printed in the USA
LVHW101915301118
598832LV00003B/4/P

9 781775 216414